A GOOD

HOUSE

IS NEVER

DONE

A GOOD
HOUSE
IS NEVER
DONE

JOHN WHEATMAN

Photography by David Wakely

Produced by Sharon Smith and Barbara Stevenson

CONARI PRESS

ISBN 1-57324-717-0

Cover and book design: Sharon Smith

Author photo: David Wakely

Composition: Deborah Reinerio

Library of Congress Cataloging-in-Publication Data

Wheatman, John
    A good house is never done / John Wheatman; foreword by Sarah Susanka.
        p.cm.
        ISBN 1-57324-717-0 3014 0692 2/04
        1. Interior decoration. 1. Title

    NK2115 . W497 2002
    747—dc21

                                                        2002067200

Printed in Singapore

02 03 04 TWP 10 9 8 7 6 5 4 3 2 1

To Gloria Learned,
the perfect friend and co-worker

For the second time, I would like to thank Sharon Smith, David Wakely, and Barbara Stevenson for making this book a reality.

I would also like to thank my talented staff: Helen Reed Craddick, Peter Gilliam, Siobhàn Brennan, Gloria Learned, Jason Collard, Mollie Womer, Sandy Wood, Brad Payton, and Diane Buzzini.

Thank you to all the skillful craftsman and contractors with whom we work—at the top of the list is Doug Leslie, whose fine lines make our drafting, I believe, the best in town.

Finally, I offer heartfelt thanks to the clients who so generously lent their homes to be photographed—Cynthia and Rob Birmingham, Jan and Thomas Boyce, Siobhàn Brennan and Durwood Zedd, Betty Ann Bruno and Craig Scheiner, Elizabeth and Jack Bunce, Louise Burns, Diane Buzzini, Helen R. Craddick, Susan and Leland Faust, Peter Gilliam and Fred Hill, Suzy and Michael Golden, John Hummer, Karen Larsen and Michael Shane, Louise and Andrew Massie, Joan and Bob McGrath, Ellen and Joerg Michelfelder, Catherine and David Post, Denise and Mark Steele, Terry and Jim Uffelman, Elsa and George Vare, and Bill Weir—and to all the others whose homes we have touched but not shown in this volume.

—JOHN WHEATMAN

The book producers offer sincere thanks to Leslie Berriman and Jenny Collins for their gracious understanding and assistance and to Diane Buzzini, Heather McArthur, Deborah Reinerio, and Cristina Rivera for their invaluable contributions.

A GOOD HOUSE
IS NEVER DONE

FOREWORD

Sarah Susanka, AIA

author of *The Not So Big House,*
Creating the Not So Big House, and *Not So Big Solutions for Your Home*

Too often, when we talk about interior design, we limit the discussion to furniture, upholstery fabrics, wall coverings, and carpet selection. A house that really expresses its owners' passions is quite another kind of interior design—one that's often difficult to express in words, but that we recognize immediately when we see. We learn much about the occupants just by being in the spaces they inhabit daily. Their lives, their loves, and their idiosyncrasies speak from the walls, and invite you in to settle and to share the experience of their world. When I came across John Wheatman's first book, *Meditations on Design,* I was delighted. Here, finally, was a book by an interior designer who knew how to communicate this. Page by page he enumerated the essential ingredients of real design, conveying the importance of imbuing each and every place with things that have meaning to the inhabitants.

A Good House Is Never Done goes further, helping readers to understand how to make a living poem out of the place they live—a poem that continues to grow and change with the years. By focusing on the basic activities that a house accommodates, such as working or sleeping, we are drawn to reconsider what we have always assumed to be the "correct" way to organize and decorate each area of the home. Wheatman asks us to question the standard, cliché solutions, and instead to invent and create

with the things we use every day, the things we love to look at, and the things we have collected over time.

As I've traveled around the country during the last few years, discussing the concepts behind my own books, I've encountered a vast number of people who are looking for a better way to live, with a far more intimate sense of home at its core. My books describe the way to shape the house, and John Wheatman's describe how to organize and personalize the house, but both are essentially aspects of the same message; namely, that good design fits the function it's put to, expresses much about its owners, and exudes the simple joy of living. Peel away the conventions and look at how you really live. Forget about keeping up with the Joneses. Look around you, become an observer of the things that bring you pleasure and that give your life meaning. Then rethink your home with those things in mind. It sounds easy, but it takes some guidance from an expert to walk you through the process. And that's exactly what this book offers.

With each page you'll discover a new trick, or a different way to think about an everyday activity, that will help transform your house into a place filled with that timeless quality of home. Far from the static stage set that results from so many decorating efforts, John Wheatman's words and wisdom will guide you through the process of making your house into a place of inspiration, beauty, and vitality. And he'll show you that as you grow and change, your house can likewise evolve to express the new in your life, while still reflecting the passions of the past. The title says it all: A good house is never done.

A GOOD HOUSE IS NEVER DONE

Zest is the secret of all beauty. There is no beauty that is attractive without zest.

—CHRISTIAN DIOR

One day not too many months ago I bought a 300-year-old table for resale in my shop. Driving home from the warehouse where I had inspected it, I could not stop thinking about this exquisite piece of furniture. By the time I arrived I had made up my mind that I simply had to have this new acquisition for my own. My business manager was deeply unhappy with my decision and no fewer than four strong men were needed to move it into place in my home. But every bit of the effort and expense involved has been more than offset by the deep pleasure I feel every day when I use this wonderful piece.

When I made this purchase we already had a dining table that served us well for 34 years. It was beautiful, flexible enough to accommodate anywhere from two to twelve diners, and perfectly in tune with the space in which it lived. Just because something is already very good, it doesn't mean that it should never change. As I am fond of telling my students and clients, a good house is never done.

I have learned to recognize the look of panic that flits across some faces when I make this statement. After all, if you think of designing your living space as a job, whose end product is a static living space that is "done" and won't need to be revisited until the furnishings wear out in another 20 years or so, the thought of the project never being completed will understandably be a dismaying one. I believe that it's more rewarding to conceive of interior design as an ongoing engagement with the fascinating business of daily life. If you approach your living space just as you welcome each new day, with an open mind and a sense of adventure, the notion that the fun goes on forever is a welcome one.

The arrangement of this volume reflects that spirit. When we first began to discuss a sequel to my first book, *Meditations on Design*, my editors suggested that we organize the photographs into sections matching the most common areas in a house: living room, dining room, kitchen, bathroom, bedroom, and work rooms. Because I wanted to write a book that reflects my dedication to flexibility, however, I chose to name the sections not for rooms but for the activities that take place in them.

I don't believe in designing dining rooms, I believe in designing spaces in which you dine—and work, and entertain, and other things you might not have thought of yet. You cheat yourself if you design a room exclusively for one activity. What a waste of space it is to set aside an entire room for sleeping, when there's ample room for a sewing machine as well as the bed—and you might want to occasionally take your rest on the couch or window seat in the living room to boot? In writing this book, our dining room became an office on most Monday mornings for nearly a year.

When you adopt this attitude, you build what is a deeper and for me more satisfying relationship with your home than you would if you simply set up a series of rooms for specific functions, decorated them to look a certain way, and then never gave them a second thought. You claim the best spaces in your home for yourself, rather than tricking them out as formal "company" rooms that sit empty for most of the time. Similarly, you mount your best art on the walls of the rooms you use most often—including bedrooms and bathrooms. You make your home an expression of who you are, with artfully arranged displays of your personal collections, rather than an imitation of a photograph from a magazine. You never stop thinking about ways in which you can make your space work for you and the particular way you live your life.

The results of this relationship are profoundly satisfying: you have not only an attractive and functional living space but also an ongoing outlet for creative expression. I hope that you understand why it is always in a tone of delight that I declare "A good house is never done."

To know what you prefer
instead of humbly saying Amen
to what the world tells you you ought to prefer,
is to have kept your soul alive.

—Robert Louis Stevenson

playing

Humanity has advanced, when it has advanced, not because it has been sober, responsible, and cautious, but because it has been playful, rebellious, and immature. —Tom Robbins

THERE'S JOY IN PLANNING a warm and friendly space. "I've had a great time!" "This has been fun!" Being able to say words like these makes the hard work worthwhile. It's a wonderful game. It's play time.

I don't think I've ever seen a truly wonderful living space belonging to someone who didn't have fun on a regular basis. Here is a truth that children know very well but too many of us have forgotten: Play is productive.

Once you've tried finger painting, or turned a large cardboard box into a clubhouse, planted seeds and watched them grow, harvested a pumpkin and made it glow on Halloween—you've entered an area of play that rewards you with both a sense of accomplishment and the spirit to forge ahead to more adventures.

In the same way, play with your living space. Be bold. Paint one wall in your favorite color, no matter how intense a shade. If you tire of it, there is nothing simpler than reverting to off-white. Experiment. Take that long dormant idea for a new coffee table constructed out of timber salvaged from your grandmother's barn and give it a whirl. You will have the satisfaction, whenever you look at it, of remembering the fun of putting it together.

Right: This client is proud of the fact that he never spends money on anything he collects. (I think his father gave him the framed Lipchitz.)

In Plexiglass boxes mounted on the wall to the left, the major part of a large matchbook collection is massed into six striking forms. On the right hand wall, the items in a special collection of Russian and vintage matchboxes are mounted and framed so that each can be seen individually. Notice another humble yet handsome collection: the corks in the glass vase holding the branches. That red Eames chair, the perfect accent here, is a playful piece of furniture frequently referred to as the "potato chip chair."

If this were set up in the Museum of Modern Art, everyone would ooh and ah over it. It's creative, it's bold, and it's a lot of fun.

have fun

Upper left: It's not what you have but what you do with what you have that counts. This suspended fish trap enjoys a second life as an intriguing wire sculpture.

The skylight's extra-wide slat shutters help to control the light and heat. There's plastic matting underfoot, and the window wall has been opened up visually by the use of a dark color.

Lower left: This handsome fellow makes his home on a kitchen wall, where he is an arresting presence.

Right: On this staircase leading up to the "Fish Trap" the risers are covered in Formica (more durable than paint) while the steps are carpeted. The staircase appears wider thanks to the contrast between the two. And because the risers aren't carpeted, the steps themselves actually are wider. Best of all, the color of the wall adds strength and unity to the landing and gives joy to the eye.

This trim wrought-iron railing was out-and-out ugly, over-detailed with scrolls and curlicues, before we gave it a haircut. Replacing it would have cost thousands.

be bold

Right: This kitchen/family room was enriched unendingly by the removal of a large picture window that looked directly onto the street. Where once there was an ugly view of parked cars, you now have a wonderful wall for art. New sources of brightness were created with the introduction of skylights. Now this is a super space for relaxing, watching television, tray-top eating, or dining around the ancient Indian bed, used as a large coffee table.

Notice how the old things placed throughout the space create a sense of warmth: the Chinese pot turned into a lamp base, the worn basket for magazines under the table, the delightful old basket hanging on the wall to the right of the sofa.

I also love the display shelf above the refrigerator, in the right background. Double-door cabinets over fridges seldom serve any purpose better than hiding things you never use and would be better rid of. They inevitably collect dirt on their tops. It's far better to leave the space open as a shelf on which to display something beautiful.

flow

Left: The fireplace in this apartment is, unfortunately, a fake. It has been converted into a strong focal point by painting out the blocked firebox in black and adding a bold metal construction form. The weathered black-and-white buoys complete the composition.

Often in a strong rectangular room the best thing you can do is introduce a round form, as Siobhàn Brennan did with this handsome coffee table, because it is less likely to block traffic than a table with corners.

When you rent, there's no reason to cheat yourself out of having good things. Simply think about acquiring furnishings that can move with you and are flexible enough to be in another space. Investing in a custom rod with a flow of fabric is much less costly than installing shutters that must be left behind. You can have carpet, but buy it as an area rug no larger than 9' x 12', so that it's easily placed in another room. And you might want to avoid buying overly large furniture—there are some elevators that can't hold an 8-foot sofa!

27

LARGE COFFEE TABLES

All too often, people take large spaces and make them unbelievably petite because they want to bring all the furniture close together around a small table.

The oversized coffee table can be the saving grace. It becomes a pivotal point for a good room arrangement. It's a place for food, for drink, for flowers, for magazines. It's always the perfect place to rest your feet.

Constantly, people will ask for a small coffee table. Inevitably, we end up providing them with a large coffee table, or in some cases, four tables instead of one. The larger the table can be, the larger the room is going to appear.

Big tables create better flow. You can conceal floor cushions or an ottoman beneath one. You can have a buffet, a bar, a think tank…more great conversations have been had around large tables than small ones.

Almost every coffee table in our shop is oversized. We use intimate small tables (or boxes, chests, trays, or trunks) next to chairs. There is a place for many other surfaces in a room.

Small coffee tables make small rooms look smaller. I'll fight for big coffee tables until the day I die.

Left: This space, on the highest level of a multiple dwelling, allows for easy back-and-forth access between living room and deck. Though the vista is vast, the space inside is intimate. The use of dark color in the room creates warmth; it also erases any division between the interior and the deck. If you took this same space and painted the walls and window frames a light color, the visual connection between inside and out would be broken, and both the deck and the room would appear much smaller.

inside outside

Whether you have inherited them or collected them over a lifetime, whether you have been frugal or extravagant—what you have is only seen at its best if each thing has its proper place and space. When a new object, painting, or plant joins the group, you have to rearrange to make room for it. Change keeps the eye awake—it's a great game to play.

play with display

Left: I love eyebrows in rooms. The shelf that goes around the better part of this space was built to accommodate a collection of richly detailed Indian baskets.

When we started to work on this house, the couple who own it were expecting their first child. Now, their children have children. This twisted wool carpet was installed with the comment that it would never wear out—and it hasn't! It was known at the time as "wool turf," the ideal choice for sororities and fraternities.

Except for the Picasso displayed on the huge Indian chest near the windows, these clients have known every one of the contemporary artists whose work is displayed in their home.

With time, this home gets better and better—proof that a good house is never done.

collections

Right: A fireplace will often have a mantle with a large piece of art over it, which becomes the focal point for the room. With this freestanding monolith, texture is the star.

This room is alive with its owner's wonderfully youthful spirit of inquiry. For forty years she has been studying and collecting Native American arts and crafts, and in this space we skillfully blend museum-quality items with far more humble objects that are beautiful in their own way.

Few things are static in a rich space. If something stays in the same place forever, at some point you stop seeing it, so you need to move things around. The two reclining figures resting on the table in the foreground, miniature versions of welcoming benches that live in the front garden, migrate to other surfaces in the room.

focal point

Left: What do you do with your dog's leash? Finding the right place can be a tricky problem. You want a spot that is out in the open, so that anyone who is willing to take the pup for a stroll can easily locate what he needs, but canine paraphernalia tends not to make the most attractive display. Here is a witty solution that's also a great example of the thoroughly satisfying effects you can achieve when you set out to have some fun.

Far left: And what do you do with things you don't use all that often but can't bear to part with? Doors that open into closets, prettily organized, are like garden gates—you always wonder what's on the other side.

secrets and surprises

Right: Theater at your fingertips. Surround sound and light. The carpet and the rich dark color accenting the strong countertop and shelves increase the apparent size of this not-very-big room. At the same time the visual impact of the electronics equipment is diminished. The neutral fabric covering a sectional sofa (in the lower right-hand corner of this photo) balances the forceful red of the two ottomans and the wall-sized painting.

The wonderful black Chinese chest stores a fabulous collection of Christmas decorations. This is a great space to be alone in, or to share with a group of eight.

amusements

Left: Two boys on the left, two girls on the right: it's their space and they make the most of it. Check out the mirrors above the doorways.

Below: When friends spend the night, they are royally entertained in this sleepover bunkhouse.

child's play

SUMMING UP

playing

- Arrange spaces for maximum flow both within themselves and into other areas.

- Establish visual connections between indoors and outdoors.

- It's not what you have, but what you do with what you have that counts.

- Consider using round forms in rectangular rooms.

- Acquire furnishings that can move with you to another home.

- Change keeps the eye awake— rearrange things periodically.

working

I cannot believe that the purpose of life is to be "happy." I think the purpose of life is to be useful, to be responsible, to be honorable, to be compassionate. It is, above all, to matter, to count, to stand for something, to have made some difference that you lived at all.

—LEO C. ROSTEN

WALKING THROUGH A SPACE THAT I'VE DESIGNED, I cannot help but feel gratified noting the host of problems we have solved and the beauty of the accomplishment. That same deep contentment can flow from many different areas—professional life, volunteer activities, the hospitality you offer friends. There is simply nothing to equal the satisfaction of a job well done.

Why then do so many of us have inadequate and inconvenient work spaces in our homes? Too often I see home offices, laundries, studies, and project rooms that are shut off in a cramped and ugly corner of an otherwise pretty space. What a shame, when you enjoy the fruits of your labor so much, to create a space for it that makes success more difficult rather than as easy as possible!

Just as a healthy lifestyle integrates work and play into a balanced whole, a well-designed house weaves work stations and living spaces together. Why stick your desk against a blank wall in the guest bedroom when you can set up a lovely spot in the living room next to the window onto the garden? No law requires that your washer and dryer be in the basement or the garage, several flights of stairs and hundreds of steps away from the center of family life. And I have yet to hear a good reason why the handsome table in your dining room can't double as a desk during the day.

Right: This beautiful table and these comfortable and handsome chairs could as easily grace a dining room as they do my firm's offices. I bought the chest in Calvados Country. Just looking at it brings back the sweet smell of acres and acres of apple trees. It is the perfect piece of furniture for people who work with clutter, as we do. A designer's space must accommodate blueprints, samples of all sorts, and rolls of tracing paper. This wonderful piece allows us to conceal quite a bit. The painting of clouds gives an open feeling to the windowless room.

a good desk

Left: Here is one of those perfect meetings between exterior landscape and interior design. Sitting at this desk for the better part of a day, you see an ever-changing landscape that is compelling yet never intrusive. If this were my office, I'm afraid I'd never get anything done!

The matchstick bamboo shades edged with black carpet binding filter the sunlight and the view. When dusk falls, they give light to the darkness outside. Night and day, inside and out, they make all that glass warm and inviting. They also keep dirt from showing on the windowpanes.

This office is a separate building, shielded by the main house, pictured below. It has a kitchen, bath, and a perfectly concealed wall bed.

Far right: This room started out a long time ago, when the children were three in number and their parents had to find rooms for them. We took one bath and made it two, removed a ceiling to gain access to the rest of the attic, and put in a ladder-like staircase that leads up to a loft, for many years the bedroom of two girls. The space you see here, once the study hall, is now the mother's home office. She has organized a compact and efficient work space that affords sufficient storage for a reference library yet offers plenty of visual inspiration: the print above the desk is very fine, the sculptures on the counter to the left endlessly intriguing, while the rug and the basket mounted on the wall to the right, pieces from her collection, are simply marvelous.

The ingenious light fixture houses two sets of spotlights: one to shine up on the ceiling and reflect a glow over the entire room, and one to provide the desk surface with light for the task at hand. If you glance for a second in the lower left-hand corner of this photo, you will see a superbly detailed handrail that permits the display of drawings all the way down the staircase wall.

Near right: In the same house, rugs from the same collection are stacked beneath a table. Even rolled on rods, they are a treat for the eye.

passion and inspiration

Left: To the right of this loft, you can catch a glimpse of the shingled ceiling shown on page 53. This is the area that served as a children's bedroom. Nowadays this space can change six times over the course of a weekend, as grandchildren create, play, and even bunk down for naps on the futon to the right.

The wraparound desk and the built-in cabinets provide ample working surfaces yet leave sufficient floor space free for the room to remain a truly flexible one. The windows that open up and out to views all around the San Francisco Bay Area ensure a plenitude of air and light. Now here's a good example of the truth that "a good house is never done." The can lights running the length of the ceiling were the best of breed when we started this room years and years ago, but something better has since come along. Next time I'm there, I think I'll suggest a change.

working rooms

Right: This home office, next to a kitchen, houses an extra oven (the shiny black surface in the lower right-hand corner of the photo). It's big enough to take the Thanksgiving turkey, which the main oven is not.

Left: Mary and I have had this *tansu* since we were first married. Originally it hung over the table we used as a gift wrap center and did a wonderful job of keeping all the ribbons and trims tidy and accessible. Now, God forbid that the laundry shouldn't be pretty—this sturdy piece is filled with a host of things that we would be hard pressed to do without.

Below: We found a spot for this stacking unit in the living area rather than the garage, because the master bedroom level is two flights up. Many a house can enjoy more than one location to do the laundry— perhaps a compact station upstairs and a double unit down, so that the muck can stay in one place and sheets and pillowcases can be tended to in another.

Left: Peter Gilliam, when he designed this office for himself, had just become our associate in the Wine Country. Now he manages to spend most weekends here at his country house and often stays through Monday as well to work with clients in that area. This table is the same one that you see used out of doors on page 107. You couldn't have a better work surface or a more handsome chair or a better spot from which to return phone calls and catch up on paperwork.

For me, too many offices are clinical. Your eye needs a chance to rest on something beautiful, to refresh your spirit as you pause for a moment in your labors. Here you have the pleasing strength of the shuttered doors opening out to an enticing vista, the handsome egg-shaped bronze knobs adorning the interior doors in the front of this photo, and the lovely pieces of art on the walls.

light and grace

FLOATING SHELVES

Everyone has a signature technique. As a group, my associates and I have a few in common, and one of them is floating shelves. I love them, and so does everyone else in my shop.

You can take a space that doesn't have an architectural statement of any merit and with floating shelves give it line and define the space so that it says, "I am strong and perfectly proportioned and I'm really handsome." And they provide terrific storage or display space to boot. We especially like to use thick white shelves and create a contrast by painting out the background wall in a rich dark color.

At times, we mount the shelves directly onto reinforcing rods projecting from the walls. At other times, we build the unit with plywood backing and suspend it on the wall. The shelves are sturdy as anything. My colleague Helen Craddick once designed a room for a man's record collection. Now, this fellow was a broadcast personality and had every great recording ever made. Helen used floating shelves, and they did a fine job of supporting the weight of the records without overwhelming the space.

Far right: This lovely, well-used space has a Ward Bennett table that is used as a desk, with the handsome shelves behind it apparently floating in space. I love the studied casualness of the wire baskets and the metal legs of these chairs—just like high-heeled shoes. The large chest adds a warm note, while the open book extends an irresistible invitation.

Top right: The young man who used this desk had no choice but to be a good student—this setup is so nice. It has the warmth of the Shaker influence and the comfort of the perfectly proportioned chair, but it also has a generous working surface and ample storage space. It is a workspace that's just waiting for someone to be brilliant. A bed, tucked up against the wall, allows this study to convert, almost instantly, into a guest room.

Bottom right: Adequate task lighting is an absolute must. There are many options available today that are not only serviceable but beautiful as well.

Left: Frequently, we will use sliding doors to conceal or reveal spaces. In this case, the door doesn't have room to slide, but it does one wonderful thing: when it is closed, this ever-so-wide floor-to-ceiling door in a dining room covers a work area. When opened, you have both the surface of the table and a countertop for desk space, making the room into a fully functional office.

We often use the same technique to screen kitchens. You can have a door that is left open against a wall 90 percent of the time but can be closed to screen the cooking area when you are entertaining guests. When the back side of the closed door reveals a display of family photographs, you have something really special—much better than the face of a refrigerator.

Right: You could do the same thing if you have a small doorway in a relatively short wall. Mount a door to cover the entire wall, completely concealing the smaller opening. It is a great inexpensive architectural trick, and it really works wonders.

close the door

SUMMING UP

working

- Integrate work spaces throughout the home.

- Tables can be used for a variety of purposes in a number of locations.

- Bring air and light and art into your work space.

- Find a hole and fill it—situate a work area in a location (no matter how unusual) convenient to the task at hand.

- Adequate task lighting is a must.

- A floor-to-ceiling door can be a terrific way to screen your home office from view when the room is being used for another purpose.

cooking

*If I actually ran the world, I'd do it from the kitchen. It's not anything
deliberate or a statement or anything, that's just how I understand things.*

—JAMAICA KINCAID

THE KITCHEN IS THE HEART OF THE HOME, the natural gathering place,
the room that is most often and most fully used. Perhaps a memory lives on,
in some residual form, of the cooking fires our ancestors gathered around.
Who can deny that we are irresistibly drawn to this place, still the emotional
center of gravity—even though the fire is most often a pilot light buried beneath
layers of steel?

Too many contemporary kitchens are designed in a way that is more likely
to smother that primitive emotional spark than to fan it. Kitchens should be
planned for cooking, first and foremost (rather than having appearance be the
primary value). What good is a space that is beautiful to look at but has no soul?

I believe that it's important to set up your cooking space with ample
storage—appliance garages, cabinets, and drawers—so that everything has a place,
and clutter can be kept to a minimum. But you don't want to go so far in the
direction of visual perfection that nobody uses the room, for fear of marring its
beauty! You want a room that is forgiving. For that reason, I love a wood floor
in the cooking area. If you stain it to emphasize the grain, it becomes just like a
tweed coat—whatever you drop on it blends into the pattern and becomes invisible.

My favorite piece of advice to anyone who is contemplating a kitchen
renovation remains, "First, go buy yourself a cookbook and learn how to cook."

Right: I bought this wonderful bakery table in France. It was on display in our shop for one day. Two parties fought over it, and these people won. We ended up designing the whole house around it.

Throughout the space, we paid particular attention to the indoors/outdoors relationship. When you are seated in this room, you can look out the windows under the cabinets and have a stunning view of the vineyard surrounding the house.

This is the kind of room, dramatic and warm, that easily becomes the center of daily activity, the heart of the home. On the next page you will see a long view of the entire first floor of this bold house, with the kitchen at the back.

center stage

Left: Nine sets of French doors enter into this continuing space, and a wheelbarrow filled with flowers is set before whichever set of doors the hosts want their guests to enter by. (I found it in France, too.)

This huge space can be left open as it is here—making it possible to seat as many as one hundred people for dining—but you also have the option of creating privacy with a series of sliding doors. Two can completely screen the kitchen from view until—"Voilà!"—you push them open and dinner is served. The set of walls behind the bookcase on the right makes a wide hallway to the master bedroom and guest bath; yet another separates the living room from an office; and two others further divide up the house.

Throughout this entire level the floor is poured concrete. We wanted to have the look of limestone, but the price tag for such an expanse was prohibitive. We created much the same effect, at a fraction of the cost, with concrete stained gently with cow dung. Whenever you use a large amount of even an inexpensive material, it looks rich.

Right: Drinks are on the house. I've never felt that a wet bar is essential, but some of them really work. This one certainly does. The glass shelves of the cabinet have been frosted on the lower surface so as not to show dust. The mirror, from the ceiling to the countertop, and the lighting, both in the cabinet and beneath it, are marvelous touches.

The stainless steel swinging door between the kitchen and dining room, when left open, successfully conceals a washer/dryer.

Some materials require more care, but they're worth it. In this case, the black floor is a nice bit of luxury, and the stainless steel splash repeated as a kickboard forms a perfect belt between the cabinetry and the floor. A collection of breadboards, worn from past use, makes a friendly totem in this dramatic space.

great kitchens

Left: The keys to a really great kitchen are quite simple. First, hide all the electrical outlets. In this case, they're mounted underneath the cabinet and shelf. Second, have a backsplash that goes from the counter to the base of the cabinets and is easy to keep clean. Third, install a floor that doesn't show dirt and counters that will so they can be kept immaculate. Fourth, make your cabinets go all the way to the ceiling—not only to give you the maximum amount of storage but also to prevent dust from accumulating on top.

Right: This used to be a tight little room with some good pictures, a small table, and a couple of chairs. By eliminating a wall and opening up the space, we created this extension of the kitchen. It has a nice sense of formality, created primarily by the glass-fronted cabinets, the thick glass shelves within, and the mirrored splash that extends all the way to the ceiling. The mirror is repeated above the doorway, which creates a flow into the dining room.

Next page: This simple remodel, conceived with clean lines, makes for a wonderful workplace and a joyous nook in which to eat and view the garden.

clever containers

Left: My father's mother, born in New Orleans, was French to the core. Her sense of food was forever. When I was young, I loved to wander through her pantry and admire the treasures on display: crocks of fruitcake covered with white fabric, saturated in spirits; another with spring fruit, steeping in sugar and brandy, so that by New Year's Day it was a treat for the palate.

My mother's father had an equally marvelous cellar, in which you could see the bounty from his garden neatly stored. I remember the potatoes especially well, growing eyes that would be cut out and planted for the new year's crop.

These were wondrous sights for a small child, and they were a large influence on my later years.

Bottom left and right: Where do you put a sponge, a scrubbing brush, or a kitchen tool? Where do you find a place for whimsy? These two vignettes tell the story. There is no need to restrict your choice of storage containers to what you find in the kitchen department of a home decor store. Expand your horizons to embrace antique shops, yard sales, and second-hand shops. And don't forget your own attic and cellar…maybe you'll find a use for that birthday gift from Aunt Maude yet!

Right: This kitchen is all about storage. When you have a family of six children and two adults, you have an opportunity for unending clutter. It is thwarted here by garages. The door of this stainless steel one (underneath the cabinet) pulls down just like yours. About 90 percent of the lower storage is drawers: things get pulled out and pushed back. Knobs are neat and don't contribute to visual clutter. You see but a small portion of a larder, with a barn door that pushes back to reveal a space immense enough to be stocked by a small grocer.

It's a wonderful family and a wonderful kitchen.

remove clutter

TRASH

Garbage is a dirty word in today's society. While it's important to remain
aware of the amount of household waste we generate (and try mightily
to reduce the volume), the element of eye pollution demands that we do
our best to hide it from view. Out of sight does not necessarily mean
out of mind.

In the best of all possible worlds, you would be able to place all of
your rubbish—compost, recyclables, and inorganic trash—directly into
the appropriate receptacle, where it would remain until disposed of. As
a student, I designed a kitchen with a countertop mounted against an
exterior wall. In the counter was a hole, through which you could drop
kitchen scraps directly into a trash can. Access to the bin was through an
outside door, making removal to the curb for pick up an easy matter.

If you're fortunate enough to have abundant kitchen space, you might
want to consider installing a cabinet designed to accommodate individual
containers for newspapers, bottles, and cans. With such a system, when
recycling day arrived, your materials would be already sorted—an elegant
and labor-saving solution.

When limited space or less-than-ideal room configurations come into
play, plenty of workable options still remain. That wonderful old bench
sitting on your front porch could hold newspaper and cardboard inside its
box seat. Bottles and cans, when stored in an intriguing box or a handsome
basket, are no longer ugly eyesores but part of attractive design elements.
The good-looking flour bin in the photo opposite is a trash receptacle.

Left: This is a corner of our kitchen. We've been in our house for a quarter of a century, and I am still changing things. A few years back, when I saw Mary on her hands and knees rummaging around for a saucepan in the bottom cabinet, I saw a chance to make things easier for her and got rid of the doors and put in drawers. I've used the same Victorian hardware in three homes. The countertop is Colorcore, a dense form of Formica that is elegant but cheap.

Right: There's no reason that storage space cannot be beautiful. The interiors of these cabinets are painted black, which provides a handsome contrast to the white china. On the lower level, black shelves and glass doors like the ones you might have in a shower give a floating look to the things stored within. Everything doesn't have to match, either—there are five different types of knobs on the doors and drawers in our kitchen.

change is good

SUMMING UP

cooking

- A warm and inviting kitchen can become the heart of the house, the center of daily activity.

- For a clean and polished look, conceal electrical outlets by putting them beneath cabinets.

- If your backsplash runs from the counter all the way to the base of the cabinets, it will be a lot easier to keep clean.

- Install a floor cover that won't show dirt.

- Extend your cabinets all the way to the ceiling so that no dust can accumulate on top.

- There is no reason why your storage spaces cannot be beautiful.

- Think about replacing lower cabinets with drawers.

dining

One cannot think well, love well, sleep well, if one has not dined well.

—Virginia Woolf, *A Room of One's Own*

I HAVE ALWAYS AGREED WITH THOSE who locate civilization in the territory of how we do things, rather than what we do. The architecture of human existence—eating, working, sleeping, and so forth—is and has been essentially the same for all people, throughout time and around the world. It is when a society advances to the point at which those basic activities are carried out with some degree of grace and art, rather than at the level of barest necessity, that the line between barbarism and civilization is crossed.

Today, when daily events may cause us to wonder how far past that line we have actually moved, dining is the arena of daily life in which we can most effectively affirm our claim to civilization. The difference, after all, between sharing a meal and merely nourishing the body is not a matter of money or time so much as it is one of care and attention. Eating food out of take-out containers in front of the television set does not save a significant amount of time, compared to having the same meal while seated at a table with cutlery and candles—rather, it costs us a great deal of things more important than the odd fifteen minutes here and there.

The daily dinner ritual might be one of the most essential arts of living well, but mealtime entertaining has to be among the most creative. I think of the theater whenever I plan a dinner for friends. I set a beautiful table, invite an interesting assortment of folks, serve them a delicious meal…and wait for the drama to unfold. I'm rarely disappointed.

Right: From the moment you enter this front gate, your sense of anticipation builds. Your path is illuminated with a wonderful sense of drama. On the patio, a table with softly glowing lights holds the promise of good food, good wine, and good company.

The welcome that you feel is also in details you might not notice: the light fixture that is large enough to attract and keep bugs at bay but not so big as to overwhelm you; the flowers on the table, cut in the morning, left in deep water for the day, and arranged at the very last moment; the bottle of wine, perfectly chilled yet already opened.

The sound of your footsteps on the gravel path eliminates the necessity of door chimes, but you know bells are going to ring before the night is over!

create
atmosphere

Far left: Kitschy kitschy koo…if you love it, there's a place for it. These porkies, leading you in to a good night of feasting, are ample proof that it's not what you have, but what you do with what you have that counts.

Left: I had a friend, long gone but much remembered, with a wonderful sense of style. When you sat at her table or walked through her rooms you would notice that hardly anything matched. But she put everything together in such a fabulously creative fashion that you could hardly wait to be invited back.

mix and match

Left: This wonderful wine cellar was once a swimming pool. We decided to locate a new home on top of it, and so reinforced and strengthened the pool, brought in two entrances and made it one of the Wine Country's talked-about cellars.

On a warm summer day, when it's too hot to be alive outside, what could be better than walking down a flight of stairs into this magic? Surrounded by bottles, you could have a meal here that would be as intimate as in the most romantic of Italian restaurants. Yet there is also a strong sense of theater. Notice how the mirror in the far left-hand corner takes the wine rack into infinity. The same thing happens on the right side, with the mirror behind the Chinese altar table. It's a big enough wine cellar, but when you see it for the first time, you think it's huge.

And I love the detailing we did to the ceiling. This is a room that's always waiting to give its best to you.

wine with dinner

Near right: Mary and I were surprised, when we first moved into our place, to find this Mafia-esque safe at the back of a closet. The only time we ever attempted to use it was when we were setting out on a trip of several weeks. We filled the strongbox from top to bottom with our most treasured possessions. The cab was waiting at the door to take us to the airport when we discovered that we had misplaced the combination! Fearful of being unable to open it again, we left the door ajar—with all of our valuables conveniently gathered in one location for any thief to find. Since then we have used the inside of the safe to store rollaway cots and other large items. We installed a motor in the ceiling to pull in cool air, so that the closet now makes a decent place for wine storage, with an attic-like loft above.

Far right: In a corner of Helen Craddick's kitchen, this champagne rack takes care of her wine storage. I love this portrait of her, done years ago—it continues to reflect her inner strength and character.

stash

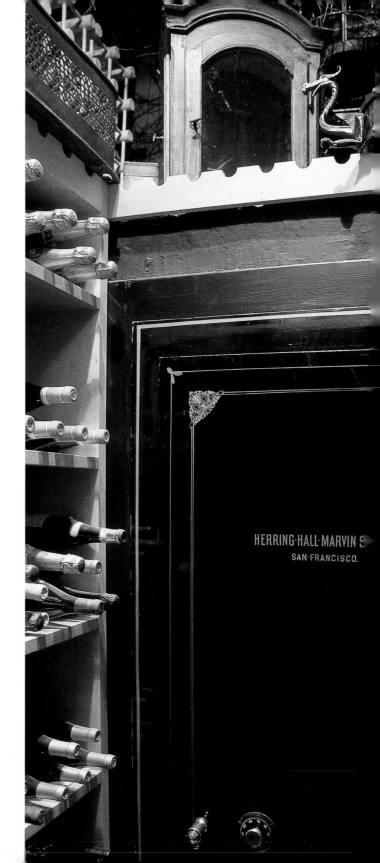

Top left: This table is in a passageway leading to a main living space. It has many moods. It can be a desk, a workspace, the perfect platform for the *New York Times*. Yet it can accept two leaves, grow 44 inches, and seat twelve for dinner. I enjoy the detailing on these chairs, especially the manner in which the pads are tied to the backs of the chairs. Compare this quiet detail to those ding-dong tassels used far too often for the same purpose!

The bookshelves reflected in the mirror demonstrate how a dark background can subdue what might otherwise appear cluttered. And it's wonderful how a simple vase with branches or cut flowers or autumn leaves can give an instant sense of time and place to a room. When the background is quiet, the joy of the change of seasons is easily felt.

Note the clean line of the metal surround of the fireplace. Too many people make the mistake of cluttering up their hearth with an overly decorative set of fireplace tools that spend most of their time collecting dust. You will probably want a poker close at hand, especially if it is as delightful as this fellow. But the other items—a fireproof metal box for sometimes hot ashes, a whisk broom, and a dust pan—can live in a utility closet and make their appearance only when pressed into service.

Bottom left and above: This warm and wonderful table could easily have been much admired and rarely used, for fear of damaging a museum-quality piece. We created an indestructible Formica slipcover, lined in felt, for it. The owners can now enjoy its beauty as a part of their everyday life. When the cover is not in use it lives propped against a wall in a long hallway, where it creates an imposing sculptural presence.

be flexible

Right: In this case, we gutted an area that was used for wine, dish, and kitchen storage. We opened up the space, pushed a wall out three feet, and made a room in which a family of eight can comfortably gather.

We also lightened and brightened things considerably with maple floors and stainless steel appliances and backsplashes. The two-sided cabinets, practical and pretty, don't block any of the light. The handsome granite countertop also serves as an ever-important place to play. I always feel great satisfaction in acquiring tables like this one—used and abused and then brought back to purposeful life.

It's all right off the garage, the garden, and the dining room. What could be better?

expand

TABLES

Worldwide, furniture design began with a box, in which you could pack and carry your treasures. With the development of tools and the availability of a wider range of materials, the box became more sophisticated. A back was added, and it became a chair. When the back was laid flat, it was a table. And so it went, on and on through the ages. The chest was thus the beginning of the table as well as the chair.

Tables were a ceremonial form, associated with all the pageantry of dining. Today, too many people make the mistake of allowing themselves to be confined by that formal heritage. They invest in as big and handsome a table as they can afford and place it in the dining room. Then they jam as many chairs around it as will fit— and they never use it! They eat their meals at an intimate counter or in a cozy corner of the kitchen.

You would do far better to find a really pretty table with a pedestal base, the kind that affords you the leg room to squeeze a few more people in when circumstances warrant. You don't need any more seats around it than you have people in your family. Invest in some comfortable occasional chairs and scatter them throughout your home where they can be put to good use on a daily basis. Then, when you need to seat a crowd for a holiday dinner, collect all the chairs you need to supplement the four or so you regularly use for dining, and everyone can be happy. Doesn't that sound like a better plan than going into debt to buy a fancy dining room set that you'll use only once a year?

After all, tables are the ultimate in flexible furniture—useful for a variety of purposes, available in a host of sizes and shapes. Expand or shrink a table by adding or subtracting leaves. Double the size of your dining room table with the addition of a collapsible top that you store under the sofa or in the window seat. I've always liked flip-top tables because they occupy so little room. I have used one that's only 18" wide and 6' long but flips open to a full 36". If you have two such models, you can make up a very handsome 6' square table when the need arises.

I might be a chair person above all, but I'm a table person after that.

Right: On page 59 we speak of Peter Gilliam's desk. Here we see the same table playing another role, superbly.

One of the joys of a country house is the ability to spontaneously decide, when the fancy strikes you and the light is just so, to move outside for breakfast or to simply bask for a while in the sun. This house, constructed in three stages—main house, guesthouse, pool and gardens—is designed to make those moments happen as often as possible, since all doors lead out to the deck and pool.

These wonderful chairs from Spain are lightweight and portable enough to encourage impromptu alfresco lunches yet comfortable enough that you will be happy to linger over a glass of wine or settle in to watch the sun set. And in case a cool evening breeze should come along, you might want to have a stack of shawls nearby to hand around so that everyone can enjoy the night a little longer.

alfresco

privacy

Left: If I should ever build a house, one of the first things I'd do is construct a fence a fair distance from the property line and then build one on the property line. In between the two, I would plant very heavily, so that I would always be able to control the garden view beyond "the property line."

That's precisely what we did here. Shortly before an important festive occasion, these clients called us in distress: their neighbors had just cut down the trees that provided a screen between this deck and their yard. We constructed a fence and a shelf, onto which we placed potted bamboo. The shelf gave height, so that the plants could provide adequate screening. Bamboo is a good choice for this purpose, since it grows so fast. The containers prevent it from getting out of control and taking over your whole yard. The other benefit of using potted trees is the simplicity of replacing one should it become diseased.

With the bamboo screen in place, this is a wonderful spot for any meal.

SUMMING UP

dining

- When you pay attention to the small but essential details, the simplest meal becomes a special occasion.

- With chairs that are lightweight and comfortable, you will be able to decide on the spur of the moment to make your meal an alfresco one.

- A good table makes a good desk: furniture that can do double duty makes living spaces graceful as well as functional.

- Whenever possible, try to create a sense of flow between and among the dining, cooking, and living areas.

- Mixing and matching—both silverware and chairs— is a wonderful way to create visual interest and achieve flexibility.

sleeping

I divide my time as follows: half the time I sleep, the other half I dream. I never dream when I sleep, for that would be a pity, for sleeping is the highest accomplishment of genius. —Søren Kierkegaard

DESIGNING SPACES FOR SLEEPING is always a challenge. There is the need for all the members of the family to have places to call their own every night, naturally. I remember working diligently once for a client whose children were fast becoming self-possessed young adults. We expended a great deal of effort and did an unbelievable amount of planning to provide spaces for all three daughter's beds. Shortly after the project was finished, the young ladies went on a trip to India together, and none of the three has ever slept in a bed again!

Sometimes your sleeping area also has a daytime job—as an office or nursery, for example. In those cases, you will want to set up as many things as possible for double duty: your bed, if it has a tailored bedspread, will make a fine surface for spreading out paperwork during the workday; and the top of a low-rise dresser will do splendidly as a changing table.

And then most of us want to be able to offer hospitality to friends and family— many of whom will consider a comfortable sleeping place an essential amenity. Here is where necessity will call forth inventiveness. Once, during an event-filled summer in my youth, my room was commandeered for guests and I slept out of doors. (I was not a happy camper.)

With summer cabins or second homes in exotic locales, it is almost inevitable that your house, which is more than sufficient for your small family, will experience the occasional invasion of overnight guests. For that reason, I will often convert one bedroom of a vacation home into a bunkhouse for as many as eight people. I suppose I've never really gotten over that long-ago night I spent on the hard ground.

Right: I enjoy tailored bedspreads. When you have one, it becomes the easiest thing in the world to crawl out of bed and restore complete order—you merely pull the covers up (and perhaps smooth them out a bit) and replace the pillows. There you have it: a clean and elegant line that never fails to please.

Compact or large, sleeping areas usually require more than a bed. You need room for your morning exercise—and maybe you need the video player, too. Often the bedroom doubles as the office, and in many lives it is the nursery. The cat likes the foot of the bed, and the children diddle as they wait for parents to play. If the initial approach is one of tailored neatness, you will have a space that is not only easy to put back into shape but also accommodating to an assortment of needs.

tailored neatness

Above: Most people I know feel as if they don't have enough closet space. I am forever trying to persuade clients to take out their closets and replace them with other forms for storage—a Japanese *misuyu*, a trunk, or a basket underneath the table. The chest shown here does an excellent job of concealing a heating register at the bottom while providing attractive storage for a television set.

People with allergies, who can't live with carpet, often fret that their rooms appear cold. This need not be the case. Here, the duvet cover and the tailored dust skirt, along with the woven wood at the windows and the pattern of the louvered doors, soften the space so that you don't think about the bare floors.

Far left: With their children grown, the couple who own this bedroom are adjusting to a new life in an apartment that is far different from their family house. Usually, you would see the cabinets at the right-hand edge of this photo in a kitchen. Yet here they cover just about one entire wall of the bedroom—providing shelves for sweats and sweaters as well as drawers for virtually anything else you can think of. And it's all a lot more accessible than a crowded closet would be.

I am fond of sharp contrasts between dark paint and light wood. Notice how the dark baseboard of the cabinet cuts the weight of the chest and makes it appear to float. The locker at the end of the bed is a neat form for storage and a good place to put up your foot and tie your shoe.

I love the expertly detailed bed frame, done in suede, with perfectly spaced nail heads. If patience is your virtue, this could be a terrific do-it-yourself project.

forget closets

Right: At the very least, window treatments filter light and provide privacy. At their best, they can have the same kind of impact that a great stage set does: they produce a mood and a storyline. Here the light, filtered by the blinds, provides a perfect complement to the Zen-like quality of the collages, which hold your attention yet don't overpower the space.

It's not necessary to have matching tables or chests on either side of the bed, or lamp bases in the form of boys and girls with holes in their heads to support the shaded light bulbs, or prints of ballerinas above the headboard—two for a double, three for a queen. Bedrooms can express personality far beyond what's available as a set in a furniture store.

catch the light

Left: Often, the first thing a property owner should do is hire a goat to tame the underbrush and a tree shaper to trim the forest, for the sake of safety as well as beauty. Here is a good example of how well-manicured greenery outside can complement an interior space—in this case, a great guest bedroom.

Visitors need a comfortable space and appointments like this charming outdoor table, to which they can retire for private relaxation. (Nobody wants to feel as if his hosts are tripping over him every time they turn around!)

Basics are also important: room to store clothes in a bureau or closet, space on the bathroom shelves for toiletries, two decent pillows per person, a good bedside reading lamp, a clock radio. If you leave out a selection of guidebooks and brochures about your favorite local attractions, along with bus and train schedules, your friends and family will be able to feel independent when staying with you.

The addition of fresh flowers is a perfect welcoming gift. No chocolates on the pillows—you don't want your company to stay too long!

guest rooms

NAPPING

My father introduced me to a very good friend, who was, I believe, the laziest man in the world. He owned some land in the Delta area. At one edge of his property he had a boat in the water and at the other a sturdy vehicle. In between was a magnificent double row of poplars, with a hammock strung between each pair of trees. When he became tired and wanted to sleep, he never had to walk any distance to do so. I found that quite impressive.

No hammock available? In my case, the sofa in the living room will always do nicely. If it's a hot, hot day, there's no better place than the leather couch in the sitting room off the garden. I firmly believe that every home needs a variety of spots, inside and out, that are conducive to short restorative slumbers. And bedrooms don't count for this sort of thing—somehow, catching forty winks isn't the same when you're doing it where you take your evening rest.

Window seats, sofas, chaise lounges, hammocks…perhaps some comfortable floor pillows and a warm blanket—how delightful to be able to choose from among a number of cozy nests.

Sleeping spaces tucked into rooms used for other purposes are wonderful.

Left: In this comfortable spot, near at hand to the fireplace, it would be all too easy to drift peacefully off. The octagonal table, by the way, has carved into the sides the names of all six children as well as the parents brought together in a blended family—a statement of faith in their future together.

Bottom: This floating window seat, which happens to be in a dining room, could as easily be in any number of spots: in your bedroom, your sewing room, a corner of the big room you've turned into a bathroom. It's a nice space.

retreats

SUMMING UP

sleeping

- Provide spaces where out-of-town guests can retreat for private relaxation.

- Equip guest rooms with not only the basics essential to comfort but also the extras that say "Welcome."

- In cases where space is at a premium, set up accommodations for guests in rooms you use for other purposes.

- Window treatments in the room where you sleep are especially important—they can filter the morning light and provide an all-important sense of privacy.

- Consider removing closets and replacing them with other forms for storage.

- When you take a tailored approach to bed linens, it is often quite easy to straighten up.

- Find spots throughout your home for napping.

bathing

There must be quite a few things a hot bath won't cure, but I don't know many of them. —S<small>YLVIA</small> P<small>LATH</small>, *The Bell Jar*

WE ALL RECOGNIZE OUR SOCIAL RESPONSIBILITY for personal hygiene, but people who know how to live well realize that when you take a purely utilitarian approach to such matters you miss out on a world of pleasures. Pampering yourself with long hot soaks and all manner of divinely scented soaps and lotions is a supremely accessible luxury—any old bathroom will do. But a well-designed space will enhance your pleasure considerably.

One of the most common design challenges we encounter in this area is the task of setting up a space for two people to share. We often will create large cabinets for storage—hoping to avoid a scenario in which someone is tripping over another's clutter. Whenever possible, we will also build private spaces into a bathroom—by screening a toilet area, for instance—so that more than one thing can be going on at a time. Even a modest space can be comfortable for two.

Since bathrooms are often relatively small, they can offer a nice opportunity to indulge yourself with small touches of luxury. Consider being more extravagant than is your normal habit when you choose wall and floor coverings. With less surface area to cover, the total cost won't be overwhelming. And think about putting some decent art in your bathroom. Too often, people reserve the best of what they have for the "public" spaces that they use the least often. I think you should have your loveliest things in the intimate areas of your home where you spend the most time.

I would also encourage you, if at all possible, to increase the size of your bathroom windows. Too often, a small window creates the sense of a small room, while a big one will produce a sense of expansiveness. Building a glass brick wall is a terrific way to let in considerably more light without sacrificing any privacy.

Left and right: I never go to Rome without seeking out the ancient baths and St. Peter's Square. There is a grandeur to these man-made creations that holds my attention, in much the same way that the redwood forests of California inspire awe. When you are able, as a designer, to bring that feeling of majesty into a private home, it's really wonderful.

I love this room. The tub is complemented by a shower that we extended out into the garden. We supplemented the plantings to provide a degree of privacy—and steam certainly helps! With shorts and terrycloth robe near at hand, it is a simple matter to stretch out on the couch. After five minutes, the responsibilities and worries of families and friends fade away…and you can just enjoy yourself.

beauty
of the bath

Left: From the outside of a house, all too often you can immediately identify the bathrooms by their windows, which scream their identity with their mean dimensions and the shadow of a cleanser can. I think you should be hard pressed, when you walk around a building, to tell which room is which. It's a mistake to sacrifice light and a view that might be spectacular for some misplaced sense of privacy. When I look up at a thirty-story apartment building and note the telltale undersized frosted windows, I want to laugh. Unless they're using binoculars, who do you think is looking at you?

I especially like the thickness of the absolutely black marble counters here, echoed in the color of the tub. If you look carefully at the left-hand side of the shower, you will be able to detect a partial glass screen that swings open, rather than a door running on a track all the way across the tub. The hardware for the curved cabinet door is so subtly placed as to be almost invisible. Electrical outlets are under the sink, so that hairdryers and electric shavers and appliances of that kind can be kept plugged in and ready to use at all times, without creating unsightly clutter. The shelf on the left, which tops the shallow cabinet for toilet paper, extends beyond its form to meet the bathtub wall, carrying that nice thick line throughout the room.

Top left: We frequently use masses of mirrors in bathrooms. Mirrors invite the eye to travel and so open up what is often a small space. When you use one as a splash, bringing it all the way down to the counter, you create strong, clean lines and multiple reflections: one rose, placed in this corner, would show itself off three more times.

A few pretty touches, such as this wooden case with the charming fellow atop it, can create a big impact. And African violets are not the only plants that thrive in the moisture of a bathroom! What a shame to leave your counters sterile and anonymous, when you could create a picture as lovely as this one. I also like the way the white enameled hardware disappears into the countertop.

Lower left: Here is a bathroom with great storage. The bottom right cabinet is big and deep enough to hold toilet and facial tissue; the middle one has outlets for hair dryers and other appliances. The medicine cabinet you see reflected in the mirror is big enough for a troop of scouts.

Right: In this excellent powder room, the cabinet below the sink is painted a rich, dark color that echoes the marble counter. The kick plate at the bottom is painted an even deeper shade, which creates a feeling of expansion.

BATHROOM STORAGE

When I was fresh out of school, the man who owned the business where I'd just been hired called me into his office the moment I arrived one morning. My new boss and his wife had recently moved, and he was having a hard time adjusting to life in a seventeenth-floor apartment that wasn't completely organized. I listened to his tale of a recent evening, when he realized, at an inconvenient moment, that there was no toilet paper, and had to descend to the ground-floor storage locker to retrieve some. Once that business was concluded, all he really wanted was a stiff drink, but he soon discovered that they had run out of Scotch! When all the essentials were restocked and the weary fellow was relaxing in the dining room, his eye alit on a radiator that he suddenly realized he absolutely detested. His message to me in that morning meeting was, "Now, young man, I want you to design a large cabinet for my home that will conceal the radiator, store dozens of toilet tissue rolls on one side, and cases of Scotch on the other."

Since that time, I've always been generous with storage for toilet tissue. Putting up one holder never seems to be enough, so I will frequently put in two. Often, however, I'll skip it entirely and put an attractive basket or box of some kind near the john and fill it to the brim.

The best place for a medicine cabinet is above the door, where no child can reach it. If you're going to have a cabinet for toiletries and the like, full-length ones are the best. Small medicine cabinets, like small mirrors, just make holes in the walls.

Right: When you are making your plumbing decisions, ask yourself how you will be using a space. In this case, placing the washer and dryer in the bath was an efficient and economical move. The countertop plays a number of roles: as bathroom counter, laundry folding space, and changing table. The wonderful star was created by the talented artist Alana. There's always a spot for great art by children.

Reflected in the mirror you can see the far wall—large slabs of limestone that are absolutely gorgeous. The glass divider between the shower and tub permits the limestone to be seen as one continuous wall-to-wall plane. It also allows you, when soaking in the tub, to look out the windows. The fixed glass on the shower wall extends from ceiling to floor, but the space above the door allows a flow of steam to escape. Another practical touch: you have a hand-held sprayer as well as a wall-mounted shower head....I scrubbed your back, now you scrub mine.

multi-purpose

Left: We over-scaled this home for a former basketball player (a very nice and a very tall man), taking a three-unit apartment building and converting it into a single home. While we needed to respect the limits of bearing walls, what we wanted to do was create as much open space as possible. The bathroom you see here, on the second floor, connects to the master bedroom, a hallway, and a sitting/guest room. From the front of this long form you have a view of the street, while the back looks out onto a garden.

Separating the two counters and sinks are three floor-to-ceiling mirrored panels. The two at either end open toward the middle, creating a three-way mirror. Closed, they conceal storage spaces enormous enough to fit all the toiletries you can imagine, appliances, and electrical outlets.

The exterior walls in the toilet enclosure and behind the tub are glass brick, providing both light and privacy. The shower has clear glass doors that slide open, and a mass of greenery on a metal balcony shields the bather from the view of outsiders. How marvelous, to be able to have the experience of an outdoor shower in the heart of a city!

space and light

Left: There's nothing wrong with an old-fashioned shower curtain, as long as it is hung at the right height and is well made. It needs to be full, though—if you use ready-mades, you might want to consider putting two together to create enough volume. The double fullness acts like corrugated plastic—water runs down the folds. One curtain will be too flat; instead of running down, the water tends to sheet against the curtain, blowing it against you.

Mounting this quartz light in the mirror allows the reflection to double the illumination provided by the 300-watt fixture. The bottom-up window shade permits a clear view and privacy as you want it. Noticing the wonderful warmth this *tansu* provides, you have to wonder why people don't use them more often in bathrooms. The chest is the base of the mirror; I like the way the wainscoting continues that line where the counter ends.

Right: Here is a simple trick that creates a prettier sight than a drain stopper. Keeping the stones clean is a matter of periodically rinsing them in a bleach wash. We have one client who uses an ancient fossil for this same purpose. It's fabulous. Imagine having a water stopper that's three million years old.

SUMMING UP

bathing

- Look for ways to bring light and air into your bathroom.

- Use masses of mirrors to make the eye travel.

- Consider practical ways to use bathroom space and consolidate plumbing needs.

- Use mirrors as a splash, bringing them all the way down to the counter.

- Remember that the reflection from a mirror behind a light fixture increases the illumination.

- Don't be afraid to have big windows in your bathroom—if you are on an upper floor, who do you think can see you?

- Think creatively about how to store toilet tissue and other essentials that you will want to have ample supplies of.

- When it comes to cabinets and mirrors, bigger is almost always better.

IT'S NOT WHAT YOU HAVE…
BUT WHAT YOU DO WITH WHAT YOU HAVE THAT COUNTS

I think of a table as a miniature stage on which one sets a scene for an actor audience: The scene may be delicate, hearty, elegant, or gay, depending on the guests who are to take part in the performance.
—ANN HAGAN, *Flair Magazine*

Many of us recognize the parallels between entertaining and theater. The care we take when guests are being entertained—in the preparation and presentation of food, in the staging of our home, in our festive dress—invests the simple ritual of the daily meal with a dramatic edge that lends an agreeable spice to the evening.

Few of us, however, think to bring the artfulness we so competently achieve for company occasions into our private lives. Every day offers the possibility of daring and drama. Too often, we miss out because we are looking for big opportunities when we should be seeking the small challenges that make a large difference.

There are many things you can do to bring grace and beauty in your everyday life, and most of them are quite simple. My father would often clip a flower and put it in his lapel…just before he took out the garbage. For me, I find that there is nothing quite so nice as starting the day by trimming the sides of my shoe soles with a fresh coat of polish—a piece of grooming perfection that puts me on top of the world.

With a small amount of effort, you can train a plant to come up the side of the building outside your bedroom window—soon you could be waking every morning to the infinitely lovely pattern of a leafy shadow on your comforter. Even if dinner is Chinese takeout for two, tapers in the candlesticks your grandmother gave you as a wedding gift might still be in order.

Why would you ever choose to plod through life, when there is joy in every day, just waiting to be unearthed?